INVENTORS' SECRET SCRAPBOOK

Chris Oxlade

Crabtree Publishing Company
www.crabtreebooks.com

Author: Chris Oxlade
Editor: Kathy Middleton
Production coordinator: Ken Wright
Prepress technician: Margaret Amy Salter
Series consultant: Gill Matthews

Picture Credits:
Istockphoto: Catherine Yeulet 22t
Library of Congress: 10, 12t, 14t, 14b, 16t, 16b, 20t, 20b
NASA: 4, 24t, 24b
Shutterstock: Cover, 3d brained 22b, Eugene Berman 26, C 5b, David Davis 29b, James Hoenstine 12b, Jakub Krechowicz 5t, Tim Jenner 11, Massimiliano Lamagna 8, Galushko Sergey 18, Sgame 6b, Alex Staroseltsev 29t
Wikimedia Commons: Enrique Dans 28, Wouter Hagens 6t, Royal Air Force 27

Every effort has been made to trace copyright holders and to obtain their permission for use of copyright material. The authors and publishers would be pleased to rectify any error or omission in future editions. All the Internet addresses given in this book were correct at the time of going to press. The author and publishers regret any inconvenience caused if addresses have changed or sites have ceased to exist, but can accept no responsibility for any such changes.

Library and Archives Canada Cataloguing in Publication

Oxlade, Chris
    Inventors' secret scrapbook / Chris Oxlade.

(Crabtree connections)
Includes index.
ISBN 978-0-7787-9909-2 (bound).--ISBN 978-0-7787-9930-6 (pbk.)

    1. Inventions--Juvenile literature.
I. Title. II. Series: Crabtree connections.

T48.O95 2011   j600   C2010-905300-1

Library of Congress Cataloging-in-Publication Data

Oxlade, Chris.
    Inventors' secret scrapbook / Chris Oxlade.
        p. cm. -- (Crabtree connections)
    Includes index.
    ISBN 978-0-7787-9930-6 (pbk. : alk. paper) -- ISBN 978-0-7787-9909-2 (lib. bdg. : alk. paper)
    1. Inventions--Juvenile literature. I. Title. II. Series.

T48.O948 2011
600--dc22

                                                    2010032439

Crabtree Publishing Company
www.crabtreebooks.com   1-800-387-7650

Copyright © 2011 **CRABTREE PUBLISHING COMPANY.** All rights reserved. No part of this publication may be reproduced, stored in a retrieval system or be transmitted in any form or by any means, electronic, mechanical, photocopying, recording, or otherwise, without the prior written permission of Crabtree Publishing Company. Published in the United Kingdom in 2010 by A & C Black Publishers Ltd. The right of the author of this work has been asserted.

Printed in the U.S.A./082010/WO20101210

Published in Canada
Crabtree Publishing
616 Welland Ave.
St. Catharines, Ontario
L2M 5V6

Published in the United States
Crabtree Publishing
PMB 59051
350 Fifth Avenue, 59th Floor
New York, New York 10118

CONTENTS

All About Inventing..4

The Microscope...6

The Electric Motor...8

A Calculating Machine...................................10

The Electric Lightbulb....................................12

The Telephone...14

The Wireless Telegraph..................................16

The Vacuum Cleaner.....................................18

A Flying Machine..20

The Television...22

The Rocket...24

The Jet Engine..26

The World Wide Web.....................................28

Glossary..30

Further Information.......................................31

Index...32

ALL ABOUT INVENTING

Inside this book you'll find pages from the notebooks of some of the world's greatest inventors. Discover how they came up with their incredible ideas—from the humble light bulb to a fantastic flying machine.

Read on and maybe you'll get an idea for your own invention. If you do, be sure to make a record of it in your own inventor's scrapbook.

INVENTORS AND INVENTING

Humans have been inventing for tens of thousands of years. They started by inventing simple tools for hunting and preparing food, made from materials they found around them.

Think of inventing and you might imagine someone in a white coat suddenly getting a bright idea! Some inventions happen like this—but not many. Most are the result of years of painstaking work, making working models, testing them, and making yet more working models.

Inventions have made space travel possible.

The greatest inventor

Italian inventor Leonardo da Vinci (1452–1519) was probably the greatest inventor of all time. He filled notebooks with sketches of amazing machines. He invented a parachute, a helicopter, a tank, and even a submarine—but couldn't build any of them with the **technology** of the time.

The importance of patents

A patent is a legal document given to an inventor by the government of a country. An inventor usually tries to patent an invention. It protects the inventor's idea from being stolen by someone else. A patent usually lasts for about 20 years.

Da Vinci's sketch of an early helicopter was beyond technology then.

THE MICROSCOPE

INVENTOR: ANTONIE VAN LEEUWENHOEK

It's a very exciting time! I've discovered how to make a **microscope** using tiny glass **lenses** that I make myself at home. It's amazing, because peering through my microscope I've seen lots of tiny animals that I couldn't see before. I've decided to call them "animalcules." I'm sure nobody even knew these creatures existed before. What a discovery!

Antonie van Leeuwenhoek

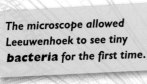

The microscope allowed Leeuwenhoek to see tiny **bacteria** for the first time.

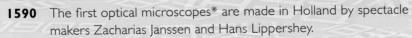

TIMELINE

1590 The first optical microscopes* are made in Holland by spectacle makers Zacharias Janssen and Hans Lippershey.

1660s Robert Hooke (Britain) publishes a book describing his observations through his own microscope.

*a microscope that uses light to **magnify** things

HOW A MICROSCOPE IS MADE   Antonie van Leeuwenhoek

1. The end of a hair-like strand of glass is put into a hot flame. The glass melts into tiny balls. These balls become the lenses of the microscopes.

2. Two metal pieces are made. Each has a small hole in the center slightly smaller than the glass ball, or lens. The metal pieces are pressed together, trapping the lens between the holes.

3. A metal pin is attached on one side of the microscope. The sharp point of the pin is directly in line with the lens.

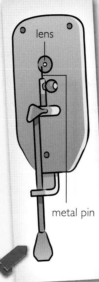

lens

metal pin

To use the microscope:

- the object that is to be studied is stuck on the pin;

- the user holds the microscope close to his or her eye and looks through the lens;

- the position of the pin is changed until the specimen can be seen clearly.

This type of microscope can show things at 200 times their normal size.

DID YOU KNOW?

Antonie van Leeuwenhoek did not actually invent the first microscope. Microscopes had been around for twenty or thirty years by the time he began making his microscopes. But he perfected a way of making lenses that produced very clear images, which he kept top secret.

1675 Antonie van Leeuwenhoek (Holland) discovers **microorganisms** by looking through his single-lens microscopes.

1938 Ernst Ruska (Germany) develops the **electron microscope**, which shows much greater detail than an optical microscope.

THE ELECTRIC MOTOR

INVENTOR: *MICHAEL FARADAY*

Electricity is the buzzword of the moment. Many of my fellow scientists are experimenting with it. Recently Hans Christian Oersted from Denmark discovered that if you put a **compass** next to a wire carrying electricity, it makes the compass needle* turn around.

I thought I could take the idea one step further and make a simple **electric motor**. And I was right!

Motors, motors everywhere

Faraday's electric motor was one of the most important inventions of all time. Hundreds of modern machines, from DVD players and electric toothbrushes to electric cars, such as the one shown right, are powered by electric motors.

TIMELINE

1820 Hans Christian Oersted (Denmark) discovers that a wire with electricity flowing in it forms a magnetic field.

1821 Michael Faraday (Britain) shows how an electric motor works.

* a compass needle is a tiny magnet

HOW AN ELECTRIC MOTOR WORKS   Michael Faraday

You will need:

- a metal dish containing mercury (mercury is a metal that is liquid at room temperature);
- a bar magnet (placed in the center of the dish);
- a piece of wire hanging loosely with its bottom end in the mercury;
- a battery with one **terminal** connected to the hanging wire and the other terminal connected to the metal dish.

What you should see:

- The end of the wire hanging in the dish will move in a circle around and around the magnet.

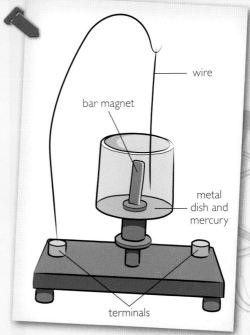

wire

bar magnet

metal dish and mercury

terminals

How it works:

1. Electricity flows from the battery along the hanging wire, through the mercury, and back to the battery.

2. The wire becomes a magnet too. Because it is a magnet, the central magnet pushes and pulls on it, making the wire move in a circle.

1837   The first working electric motor is made. It is used for powering machines in factories.

1907   James Murray Spangler (U.S.A.) uses an electric motor to power the first **vacuum** cleaner.

A CALCULATING MACHINE

INVENTOR: CHARLES BABBAGE

This inventing business is very frustrating! I've spent years designing machines that can do sums, but I still haven't managed to build one. I call them calculating machines, and I'm sure they will be used everywhere one day.

Charles Babbage

DID YOU KNOW?

Babbage was often ill when he was a child and spent a lot of time at home. His parents once told his teachers not to "tax his brain too much!"

TIMELINE

1822 Charles Babbage (Britain) begins designing his first calculating machine called the Difference Engine.

1833 Babbage begins designing a new machine called the Analytical Engine. It is far more advanced than the first because Babbage wanted it to carry out complicated sums.

PARTS OF A CALCULATING MACHINE Charles Babbage

1. A punched-card* reader. Some cards contain data (information) and some contain instructions.

2. A section that does additions and subtractions (sums), known as the mill

3. A store where the results of the sums done in the mill are stored to be used later

4. A printing section where results are printed onto paper

5. A steam engine to power the machine

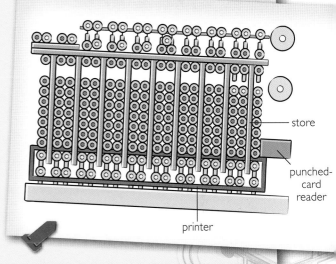

store

punched-card reader

printer

Babbage's failure

Charles Babbage's machines would have contained thousands of **cogs**, **levers**, and other small parts. At the time, these would have been tricky and very costly to make. This was one reason why Babbage never built the machines.

1871	Babbage dies without building either of his machines.
1938	Konrad Zuse (Germany) builds the first electric computer.
1991	The London Science Museum completes Babbage's calculating machine.

* the punched-card contains information for the machine

THE ELECTRIC LIGHTBULB

INVENTOR: THOMAS ALVA EDISON

Thomas Alva Edison

I've spent my whole life inventing things. I've become famous for it. I've come up with new types of telegraph machine, a microphone, and the world's first machine for recording sound. But my most famous invention is the electric lightbulb. What a bright idea that was!

Edison vs. Swan

Most people believe that Edison invented the lightbulb, shown right. But it was also invented in Britain by Joseph Swan. At first Edison and Swan argued over who should be granted the patent for the lightbulb, but in 1883 they began manufacturing bulbs together.

TIMELINE

1809 Humphry Davy (Britain) invents the electric arc lamp*, which is used for street lighting.

1878 Joseph Swan (Britain) invents an electric lightbulb.

1879 Thomas Edison (U.S.A.) invents his electric lightbulb.

* an arc lamp produced light from a powerful electrical spark

THE ELECTRIC LIGHTBULB   Thomas Edison

glass bulb

filament

terminals

The Edison lightbulb has the following parts:

1. Filament

A thin thread of **carbonized** bamboo, made by heating thin strips of bamboo without letting them burn. When electricity flows through the **filament**, it makes the filament so hot that it glows brightly. The filament is held in place by thin wires that carry electricity to it.

2. Glass bulb

The air is sucked out of a thin glass container. This makes a vacuum. The vacuum stops the filament from burning up, which would happen if there was air in the container.

3. Terminals

The terminals on the outside of the bulb are connected to the filament. They carry electricity in and out of the bulb.

1882   Edison builds an electricity **generating station** in New York to produce electricity for lightbulbs in the city.

1883   Edison and Swan join forces to make and sell electric lightbulbs.

1926   Edmund Germer (Germany) invents the **fluorescent** lightbulb.

1990s Energy-saving bulbs are introduced to replace filament lightbulbs.

THE TELEPHONE

INVENTOR: ALEXANDER GRAHAM BELL

It's true that I invented the telephone, but I was helped along by a lucky accident. I was experimenting with a new type of **telegraph** machine for sending **Morse code** messages when I heard sounds coming from it. It was incredible! This spurred me on to make a machine to send voices along a telegraph wire.

DID YOU KNOW?

In later life Bell refused to have a telephone in the study where he worked. He thought the telephone's ringing was a nuisance!

The telephone made staying in touch much easier for people.

Alexander Graham Bell

TIMELINE

1875	Alexander Graham Bell sends sounds along a telegraph wire.
1876	Bell builds the very first working telephone (Canada).
1876	Elisha Gray (U.S.A.) also designs a working telephone.
1876	Bell is awarded a patent for his telephone.

14

EXPERIMENTAL TELEPHONE   Alexander Graham Bell

You will need:

Parts for the **transmitter**:

- paper cone
- diaphragm (a thin, flexible sheet of metal)
- needle attached to diaphragm
- metal dish containing **acid**
- battery

Parts for the **receiver**:

- **electromagnet**
- metal reed

How it works:

1. The battery pushes electricity through the needle, the acid, and the dish. Then the electricity flows along a wire to the electromagnet in the receiver and back along another wire to the battery.

2. Speaking into the transmitter makes the diaphragm move up and down. This makes the tip of the needle move up and down in the acid. In turn this makes the electricity flowing to the receiver weaker or stronger.

3. At the receiver, the electricity changes how strongly the electromagnet pulls on the metal plate. This makes the metal plate vibrate up and down, creating sound.

paper cone
metal reed
electromagnet
diaphragm
needle
battery
acid
metal dish

1878   The first **telephone exchange** is opened in Connecticut in the United States.

1891   Almon Strowger (U.S.A.) invents the automatic telephone exchange, which allows callers to directly dial other people without going through an operator.

1971   The first cellular telephone network is opened in Finland.

THE WIRELESS TELEGRAPH

INVENTOR: GUGLIELMO MARCONI

Guglielmo Marconi

I've just heard my brother's shotgun fire. That was his signal to let me know he received my wireless telegraph message. It means my invention is working. I've managed to send a message using radio waves!

DID YOU KNOW?

Radio communications quickly became popular on ships for keeping in contact with the shore and other ships. As the *Titanic* sank in the Atlantic in 1912, radio operators on board sent distress signals using Marconi's new equipment.

The Titanic sent out a call for help using Morse code.

TIMELINE

1888	Heinrich Hertz (Germany) discovers radio waves.
1895	Guglielmo Marconi (Italy) sends messages using radio waves.
1899	Marconi sends radio signals across the English Channel, between England and France.

COMMUNICATION WITHOUT WIRES Guglielmo Marconi

How it works:

The transmitter

- Radio waves are sent out by a transmitter when its Morse code key is pressed down.
- A transmitter is made up of an aerial (a long wire or metal plate held in the air) connected to a special electric **circuit**.
- Inside the circuit a spark creates a powerful surge of electricity in the aerial. This sends radio waves.

The receiver

- The receiver is also made up of an aerial, like the transmitter. It picks up radio waves from the transmitter.
- When radio waves hit the aerial, they create electricity. The receiver's electric circuit picks up this electricity and sends it to a bell, making it ring.

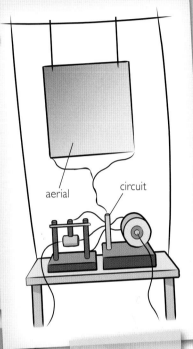

aerial   circuit

This diagram shows a radio transmitter.

A family business

Marconi began his experiments in his family's large home in Italy. Marconi's father thought he was wasting his time, but his mother gave him money to buy equipment, and his brother became his assistant.

1901 Marconi sends a radio signal across the Atlantic Ocean from England to Canada using 197-foot (60 m) tall aerials.

1906 The first successful transmission of music by radio.

1920s The first radio stations are **broadcasting**.

1930s Television is broadcast using radio signals.

THE VACUUM CLEANER

INVENTOR: JAMES MURRAY SPANGLER

I've been a furniture salesman and an inventor, but recently I've worked sweeping carpets in a department store. I suffer from asthma, and the dust from the carpets made me cough a lot. I was so fed up that I decided to make an electric carpet-cleaning machine.

Vacuum cleaners make cleaning easier and less time-consuming.

TIMELINE

1901 Hubert Cecil Booth (Britain) builds a vacuum cleaner driven by an oil engine that sucks dust through hoses.

1907 James Murray Spangler (U.S.A.) invents a portable vacuum cleaner.

THE SUCTION SWEEPER   James Murray Spangler

1. Take a **carpet sweeper** that has a spinning brush. Cut a hole in the back of the cover.

2. Find an electric motor, for example, from an electric sewing machine.

3. Put a fan on the **shaft** of the motor. Mount the motor on the carpet sweeper so that the fan sucks air out of the carpet sweeper case.

4. Place a leather belt around the shaft of the motor and the shaft of the sweeper's spinning brush.

5. Attach a pillowcase to the sweeper so that air from the fan is blown into it. The bag acts as a filter, allowing air to escape, but trapping dust.

6. Finally, add a broom handle to push the sweeper along.

Testing: Switch the motor on and push the sweeper forward. The brush should spin, and dust-filled air should be blown into the bag.

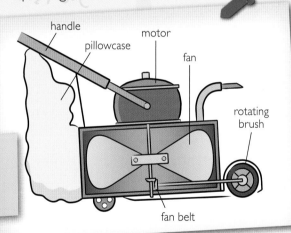

Spangler's original model of a carpet cleaner

handle
pillowcase
motor
fan
rotating brush
fan belt

1908   William Hoover (U.S.A.) begins manufacturing Spangler's vacuum cleaners.

1983   James Dyson (Britain) launches the world's first bagless vacuum cleaner, which removes dust from the air by spinning it at high speed.

A FLYING MACHINE

INVENTORS: ORVILLE WRIGHT AND WILBUR WRIGHT

Phew! My brother, Orville, has just brought our aircraft *Flyer* safely back to the ground. We've just made the first-ever successful flight in an airplane. Today is December 17, 1903. Remember this date! Now it's my turn to be the pilot...

A long road to success

The Wright brothers' success came from carrying out thousands of flight tests with kites and gliders over a period of four years before attempting to build their powered aircraft. Rival **aviators** took shortcuts and failed.

Orville Wright (top) and Wilbur Wright (bottom)

TIMELINE

1902 The Wrights (U.S.A.) complete their third glider.

1903 Orville Wright makes the first powered, controlled flight of a heavier-than-air aircraft at Kill Devil Hills, near Kitty Hawk in North Carolina.

A GUIDE TO THE WRIGHT FLYER   Wilbur Wright

- The wings are made up of a wooden frame covered with cloth.

  The curved shape of the wing creates lift, or an upward push, to lift *Flyer* off the ground as it moves forward.

- A lightweight engine drives two **propellers**, one on each wing, using chains. Propeller speed is controlled by the engine's **throttle**.

- Flight direction is controlled by moveable surfaces. These consist of:

  - **rudders** at the rear that turn *Flyer*;
  - **elevators** at the front that make *Flyer* climb and descend;
  - wing tips that twist to make *Flyer* roll from side to side.

- Levers linked to the rudders, elevators, and wing tips allow the pilot to move these surfaces to control *Flyer*.

- The take-off system consists of a trolley on a rail. Skids are provided for landing.

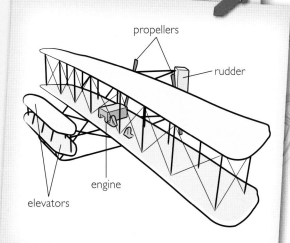

propellers

rudder

engine

elevators

1905   *Flyer III* is the first practical aircraft capable of long flights.

1969   The Boeing 747 has its first flight. Its **fuselage** is longer than the length of the Wright's first historic flight.

THE TELEVISION
INVENTOR: JOHN LOGIE BAIRD

I've invented air-cushioned shoes and a glass razor. Unfortunately, the shoes popped and the razor shattered! But I'd always loved the idea of transmitting moving pictures of events. In 1925 I built the world's first working television. Amazing! Here's how it worked...

Today, everyone can watch television because of Baird's invention.

TV history

The first television receivers were huge, but had tiny screens, just a few inches wide. Early televisions, such as this one (right), look very old-fashioned today.

Timeline

1925 John Logie Baird (Scotland) builds a television system that sends a moving image.

1926 Baird demonstrates his television system in Selfridges department store in London.

1928 Baird sends a television signal from London to New York.

HOW THE TELEVISION WORKS   John Logie Baird

The system uses a transmitter to send pictures and a receiver to display them.

The Transmitter

1. A bright light is shone on the subject.
2. A motor powers a spinning disc.
3. Light shining on the subject passes through the spinning disc. Holes divide the light into lines. This process is known as scanning.
4. Light then hits a photovoltaic cell, which is sensitive to light and reacts by sending out an electrical signal.
5. A transmitter turns the electrical signals into radio signals.
6. The signals spread through the air.

The Receiver

7. The aerial turns radio signals into an electrical signal.
8. The signal controls the brightness of a lightbulb.
9. The light from the bulb shines through the spinning disc, recreating the lines of the picture.
10. The picture appears on a small glass screen.

This diagram shows a television transmitter.

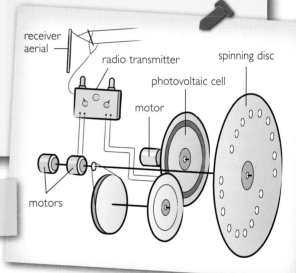

receiver aerial
radio transmitter
spinning disc
photovoltaic cell
motor
motors

1929   The British Broadcasting Corporation begins to broadcast television programs using Baird's equipment.

1950s   Color television broadcasts begin.

THE ROCKET

INVENTOR: ROBERT GODDARD

Robert Goddard

As a child, I used to dream of amazing vehicles that could take me to the stars. Today, after five years of experiments, I tested my first rocket, and zoom...up it went. I hope it's the first step on the journey to space.

DID YOU KNOW?

Not many people believed that Goddard's rockets would work. How wrong they were! Today, Goddard is known as the father of the space age.

Goddard's work made all later explorations into space possible.

TIMELINE

1045 In China, the first gunpowder-fueled rockets are used as weapons.

1926 In the United States, Robert Goddard launches the first successful liquid-fueled rocket.

NOTES ON A LIQUID-FUELED ROCKET   Robert Goddard

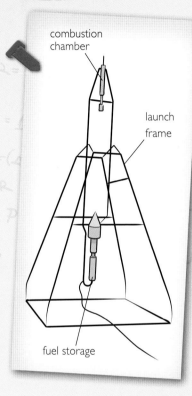

combustion chamber

launch frame

fuel storage

Use of liquid fuel

1. The flow of liquid to the engine can be adjusted, so the thrust, or push, of the rocket engine can be controlled.

2. I've decided to use gasoline and liquid oxygen as the fuels.

Fuel storage

1. Fuel is stored in tanks at the base of the rocket, gasoline in one and liquid oxygen in the other.

2. A small heater turns the liquid oxygen into gas.

3. Pipes transport fuel up to the **combustion chamber**. These pipes also form the frame of the rocket.

Combustion chamber

1. **Valves** allow gasoline and oxygen to mix in the combustion chamber.

2. The gasoline burns and produces hot gases that rush out through the **nozzle**.

Launch frame

Before it launches, the rocket is supported by a metal launch frame.

1942   Germany launches V2 rockets against Britain during World War II.

1957   A rocket lifts the first satellite, Sputnik 1, into orbit around Earth.

1969   A Saturn V rocket launches astronauts to the first Moon landings.

THE JET ENGINE

INVENTOR: FRANK WHITTLE

I used to be a fighter pilot, so I knew a plane would be able to fly higher and faster with a jet engine. I finally built a working **prototype** jet engine, but then ran out of money. At first the government didn't take my engine seriously. But when war with Germany looked likely in 1939, they came up with the cash to help me build it.

DID YOU KNOW?

Frank Whittle was a fighter pilot, flying instructor, and test pilot in the British Royal Air Force. He was once eliminated from a flying competition for flying dangerously to show off his skills.

Modern jet fighter planes are based on Whittle's work.

TIMELINE

1937 Hans von Ohain (Germany) tests an experimental jet engine.

1937 Frank Whittle (Britain) tests his model jet engine, called the W.U.

1939 Powered by von Ohain's engine, the Heinkel He 178 makes the first successful flight of a jet-powered aircraft.

A GUIDE TO THE JET ENGINE   Frank Whittle

1. Air intake
Collects air needed for fuel to burn.

2. Compressor
A high-speed spinning fan sucks air through the intake and squeezes it.

3. Combustion chamber
The air flows into the combustion chamber. Fuel is also injected into the chamber. The fuel burns, creating super-hot gases.

4. Turbine
Gases from the combustion chamber rush through sets of blades, making them spin. The **turbine** drives the compressor (see 2).

5. Exhaust
Hot gases blast out of engine here.

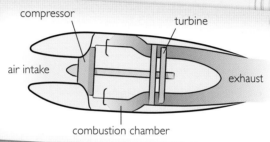

compressor

turbine

air intake

exhaust

combustion chamber

Whittle and von Ohain

Both Whittle and von Ohain rushed to perfect their fighter plane engines. But in the end jet fighters, like the one shown right, played only a minor part in WWII.

1941 The Gloster F28/39 becomes the first aircraft to fly, powered by Whittle's jet engine.

1949 The first jet-powered commercial passenger plane, the de Havilland Comet, takes to the air.

THE WORLD WIDE WEB

INVENTOR: *TIM BERNERS-LEE*

Working as a scientist back in the 1980s, I used to look at hundreds of documents stored on computers. One day I realized how useful it would be to jump from one document to another simply by clicking on some sort of link in the document. The end result was the World Wide Web!

Tim Berners-Lee

DID YOU KNOW?

Tim Berners-Lee is now head of the World Wide Web Consortium (W3C), the international organization that sets standards for the World Wide Web. Berners-Lee never made any money from inventing the World Wide Web because he wanted everyone to have access to it—not just those who paid him.

TIMELINE

1969 U.S. Government computers are linked together to share information. This computer network became known as ARPANET.

1970s The Internet was born when various other networks around the world were linked to ARPANET.

28

WORLD WIDE WEB FAQs   Tim Berners-Lee

What is the World Wide Web?

It is a huge collection of information stored on computers on the Internet (see below) in the form of Web pages. The information is in the form of text, images, video, sounds, and other data*.

What is html?

Hypertext markup language (HTML) is a computer language used to build and format documents for the World Wide Web.

What is a hypertext link?

A hypertext link on a Web page is a piece of text or an image that has an underlying code which takes the user to another Web page when clicked.

What is needed to look at Web pages?

A computer needs software to fetch and display HTML files. This is called a Web browser.

What is the Internet?

The Internet is a vast computer network made up of millions of computers around the world connected together.

1990 Tim Berners-Lee (Britain) develops hypertext markup language (HTML).

1991 The World Wide Web is launched on the Internet.

2008 The number of Web pages on the Internet reaches one trillion.

---

* Originally, it was just text.

GLOSSARY

acid Liquid that can rot materials

aviators People who fly or build aircraft

bacteria Tiny single-celled creatures

broadcasting Sending signals from one transmitter to many different receivers

carbonized Turned into carbon

carpet sweeper A mechanical device pushed by hand for cleaning carpets

circuit Loop that electricity flows through

cogs Wheels with a rim of teeth

combustion chamber Space where fuel burns

compass A device that indicates direction

electric motor Device that turns electricity into movement

electromagnet Magnet made by sending electricity through a wire

electron microscope Microscope that magnifies images of objects using tiny particles called electrons

elevator A part on the tail of an airplane, which can be controlled to help move the plane up or down

filament Thin object, like a thread

fluorescent Lightbulb containing glowing chemicals that give out light

fuselage Main part of the body of an aircraft

generating station Place where electricity is made

lenses Pieces of glass or plastic which bend light rays from an object

levers Rods that can pivot up and down or from side to side

magnify Enlarge to an extreme measure

microorganisms Plants and animals that are so small you can't see them without using a microscope

microscope Device used to look at tiny objects in detail

Morse code Code in which letters are shown by dots and dashes

nozzle Hole that gas comes out of

propellers Fan-shaped objects that spin to push or pull an aircraft

prototype Early working version of something

receiver Device that turns signals back into sound

rudder A flat piece of metal at the rear of an airplane, used for steering

shaft A cyclindrical bar used for support

technology Scientific information that tells people how to build or make something

telegraph Machine that sends written messages using electricity

telephone exchange Place where telephone lines from different houses are connected together

terminal One of the two metal connections on a battery

throttle Handle that controls the speed of an engine

transmitter Device that turns sound into an electrical signal

turbine Set of fans that spin at high speed when gas rushes past them

vacuum Place where there is nothing, not even air; used to create suction for devices, such as a vacuum cleaner and a lightbulb

valve A device that controls the flow of materials

FURTHER INFORMATION

WEB SITES

The Thomas Edison National Historical Park, New Jersey, has a lot of information about Edison on its Web site at:
www.nps.gov/edis/index.htm

Read more about the Wright Brothers on the official Web site at:
http://wrightbrothers.info

There is an interactive site about Marconi at:
www.marconicalling.com

Read a biography of Alexander Graham Bell with links to other Web sites about him at:
www.alexandergrahambell.org

Read about some of Leonardo da Vinci's fascinating inventions at:
www.mos.org/sln/leonardo/InventorsWorkshop.html

BOOKS

The Story of Inventions by Anna Claybourne and Adam Larkum. EDC Publishing (2007).

Breakthrough Inventions Series. Crabtree Publishing Company (2007).

Inventions and Inventors by Darren Sechrist. Crabtree Publishing Company (2009).

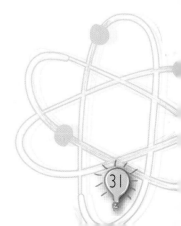

INDEX

acid 15
aircraft 20–21, 26–27
aviators 20

Babbage, Charles 10–11
Baird, John Logie 22–23
battery 9, 15
Bell, Alexander Graham 14–15
Berners-Lee, Tim 28–29

calculator 10–11
carbonized 13
circuit 17
cogs 11
combustion chamber 25, 27
computers 11, 28–29

da Vinci, Leonardo 5

Edison, Thomas Alva 12–13
electricity 8–9, 12–13, 15, 17, 23
electric lightbulb 12–13, 23
electric motor 8–9, 19
electromagnet 15
engines 11, 21, 26–27

Faraday, Michael 8–9
filament 13
fluorescent 13
fuselage 21

generating station 13
Goddard, Robert 24–25

Hoover, William 18, 19
HTML 29

jet engine 26–27

lenses 6, 7
lever 11

Marconi, Guglielmo 16–17
microscope 6–7
Morse code 14, 17

nozzle 25

patent 5, 12, 14
propellers 21
prototype 26

radio signals/waves 16–17, 23
receiver 15, 17, 22, 23
rocket 24–25

sketches 5
Spangler, James Murray 9, 18–19
steam engine 11

technology 5
telegraph 14, 16–17
telephone 14–15
television 22–23
terminal 9
throttle 21
transmitter 15, 17, 23
turbine 27

vacuum 13
vacuum cleaner 9, 18–19
van Leeuwenhoek, Antonie 6–7

Whittle, Frank 26–27
World Wide Web 28–29
Wright brothers 20–21